SEATTLE WALK REPORT

SEATTLE WALK REPORT

An Illustrated Walking Tour
through 23 Seattle Neighborhoods

Susanna Ryan

SASQUATCH
BOOKS
SEATTLE

Printed in Canada

SASQUATCH BOOKS with colophon is a registered trademark of Penguin Random House LLC

23 22 21 20 19   9 8 7 6 5 4 3 2 1

Editor: Jennifer Worick
Production editor: Bridget Sweet
Production designer: Tony Ong

Library of Congress Cataloging-in-Publication Data
Names: Seattle Walk Report (Cartoonist), author.
Title: Seattle walk report : an illustrated walking tour through 23 Seattle
   neighborhoods.
Description: Seattle, WA : Sasquatch Books, 2019.
Identifiers: LCCN 2019003237 | ISBN 9781632172617 (hardback)
Subjects: LCSH: Seattle (Wash.)--Guidebooks. | Seattle (Wash.)--Tours. |
   Seattle (Wash.)--Comic books, strips, etc. |
   Walking--Washington--Seattle--Tours. | Graphic novels. | BISAC: TRAVEL /
   United States / West / Pacific (AK, CA, HI, NV, OR, WA). | TRAVEL / Hikes
   & Walks. | SPORTS & RECREATION / Walking.
Classification: LCC F899.S43 S44 2019 | DDC 917.97/77204--dc23
LC record available at https://lccn.loc.gov/2019003237

ISBN: 978-1-63217-261-7

Sasquatch Books
1904 Third Avenue, Suite 710
Seattle, WA 98101

SasquatchBooks.com

CONTENTS

Introduction   vi
Welcome to the Neighborhoods   1

Ballard   2
Capitol Hill   12
Central District & Leschi   22
Chinatown-International District   32
Downtown   42
Fremont   52
Green Lake, Wallingford & Phinney Ridge   62
Lake City & Wedgwood   72
Madrona, Madison Park & Montlake   82
Pioneer Square   92
Lower Queen Anne   102
Upper Queen Anne   106
Rainier Beach   112
SoDo & Georgetown   122
West Seattle   132
The Eastside   142

Conclusion   151
Search & Find   154
Walking Supplies   158
Index   160
Acknowledgments   165

The book you hold in your hands is not a Seattle walking guide. Not exactly. Inside, you won't find the coolest secret spots from which to view Mount Rainier or the best routes around Seattle's streets. This book is instead a call to explore and to celebrate the overlooked everyday marvels that surround us.

I haven't always been a walker. I come from a long line of people more likely to break world records in Tetris than in team sports. Only a few years ago it would take me all day to muster up the enthusiasm to walk half a mile to the grocery store up the street.

It was love at first sight when I laid eyes on this carrot with a straw through it on Capitol Hill.

In 2017, I noticed a pair of Mr. Potato Head toys hanging on a wire over the Jose Rizal Bridge.

NO, THANK YOU!

When I saw this pool chair surrounded by seven of the same shoe during a walk in Seattle's southern neighbor Fife, I hopped on a bus and left!

One day, that all changed. On a whim, I left my apartment in the early morning and started walking without a destination in mind. Almost like magic, Seattle began revealing itself to me in ways I had never taken the time to see before. Streets I thought I knew well turned into opportunities for delightful new discoveries. Slowing down and being open to possibility allowed me to see my city in a different way, and suddenly everything I saw—from sidewalk trash to tiny parks—seemed remarkable. Walking became my passion. I realized that I didn't need money, a car, or a week off from work to see new and fabulous things. There was an entire world hiding in plain sight in my own hometown.

A desire to share these discoveries with other people led me to combine my newfound love of walking with my lifelong passion for drawing in an Instagram comic I called "Seattle Walk Report." The growth of my readership led to the opportunity to create this book, which contains all-new comics based on all-new walks through Seattle's neighborhoods.

This book is divided up into 16 parts, each one chronicling a walk I took through a different part of Seattle. Some of the longer walks spanned several neighborhoods, while some of the shorter walks were concentrated in just one. Each section includes a map of the route I happened to walk on that particular day, but if this book inspires you to get out and explore Seattle's neighborhoods, you don't need to follow my path step-by-step. My hope is that you'll use this book as a jumping-off point to inspire adventures all your own and pursue whatever catches your eye.

Or, if you don't feel like going outside ever again, that's OK too. I'm not the boss of you.

Seattle Walk Report

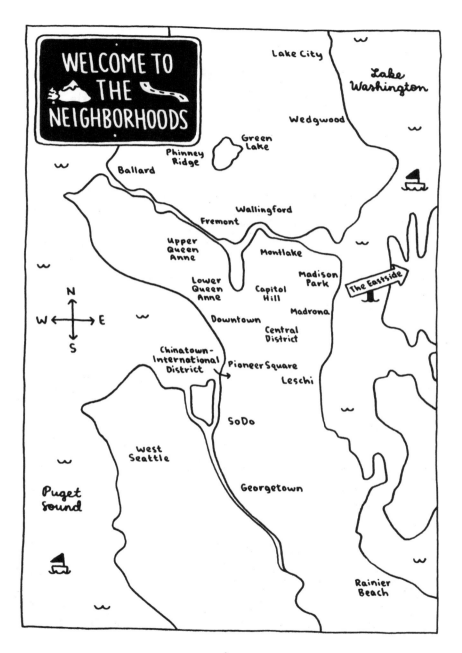

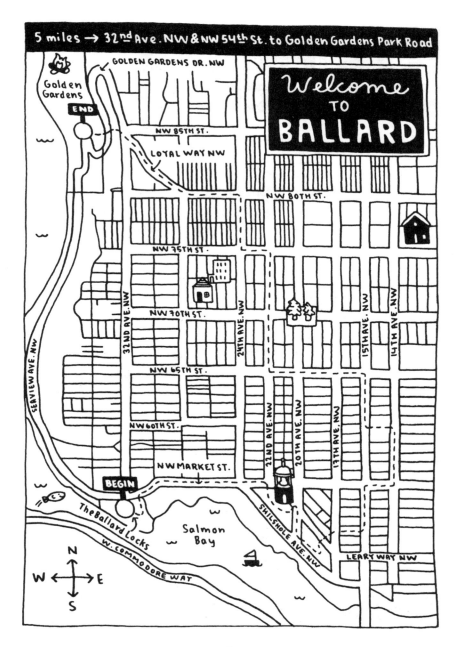

Ballard
Ballard is a large neighborhood with no shortage of great walking opportunities. It's a patchwork of new and old buildings, residential and commercial areas, waterfront views, and tree-lined streets. Beginning a walk on a main street like Market and heading in any direction is sure to lead to a nice afternoon.
If you walk here, be on the lookout for:
☑ interesting side streets
☑ views of the water
☑ a mix of old and new houses
☑ Scandinavian flags

5 miles → 32nd Ave. NW & NW 54th St. to Golden Gardens Park Road

Golden Gardens

END

GOLDEN GARDENS DR. NW

NW 85TH ST.

LOYAL WAY NW

NW 80TH ST.

Welcome TO BALLARD

NW 75TH ST.

NW 70TH ST.

NW 65TH ST.

NW 60TH ST.

NW MARKET ST.

BEGIN

SEAVIEW AVE. NW

32ND AVE. NW

24TH AVE. NW

22ND AVE. NW

20TH AVE. NW

13TH AVE. NW

15TH AVE. NW

14TH AVE. NW

SHILSHOLE AVE. NW

LEARY WAY NW

The Ballard Locks

Salmon Bay

W. COMMODORE WAY

N
W ← → E
S

3

HOUSES FOR SALE: ~~||||| |||||~~ ~~||||| ||||| ||||| |||||~~ ||||

JAYWALKERS: ~~|||||~~ |

MANHOLE COVER

A piece of Ballard history at your feet!

SALMON BAY FOUNDRY CO.

These manhole covers can be found throughout Seattle, but they're a Ballard original! The Salmon Bay Foundry operated in Ballard from the early 1900s until the mid-1970s.

The Ballard Bell built in 1892

OOH! A row of knocked-over newspaper boxes!

THERE WAS A REAL-LIFE
BALLARD BEAVER AT
GOLDEN GARDENS!

LOCKS OF THE BALLARD LOCKS

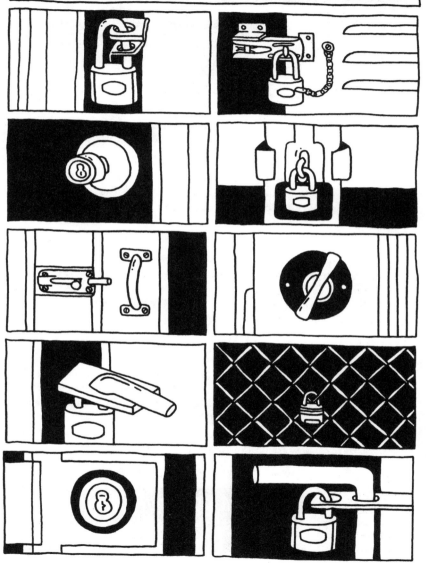

Mom's MARKET ST Memories

My mom, a rare Ballard native, shares her top childhood spots on Market St.!

```
22ND AVE. NW  ① ②  20TH AVE. NW      13TH AVE. NW       15TH AVE. NW    14TH AVE. NW
         NW MARKET ST.    NW MARKET ST.   NW MARKET ST.   NW MARKET ST.
         LEARY  RUSSELL   TALLMAN  BARNES                              ③
```

⭐1 <u>THEN</u>: The Bay Theatre   <u>NOW</u>: Majestic Bay Theatres
"When first-run Disney movies would come to town, the line
to see them at the Bay Theatre would stretch around the
freakin' block. I would dig money out of the couch for
admission (50¢), and for an extra 25¢, I could get both pop
and popcorn."

⭐2 <u>THEN</u>: The Ballard Library   <u>NOW</u>: Kangaroo & Kiwi pub
"Visiting the old Carnegie Library was my first memory on
earth. I remember the wonderful children's librarian and,
at age 3, feeling so small surrounded by tall shelves of books
in the big round room. The smell of hardwood has stuck with
me all these years."

⭐3 <u>THEN</u>: Pay'n Save and Tradewell   <u>NOW</u>: Safeway
"Pay'n Save, a drugstore, and Tradewell, a grocery store, were
connected in a building between 14th and 15th. Everyone would
line up to see [local TV stars] J.P. Patches and Gertrude when
they made promotional appearances at Pay'n Save. When we were
older, we would buy issues of "16" and "Tiger Beat" magazines
there along with our 45s. That Pay'n Save was like our teenage
mall before anyone could drive."

FREE FINDS

just the bottom part of a chair on NW Leary Way

a floral ottoman on NW 70th St.

a dresser on NW 59th St., only missing two drawers!

a broken mirror on NW 65th St.

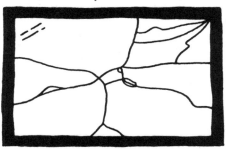

FREE!

a box of karate trophies on NW 80th St.

PARKS NAMED AFTER

URSULA JUDKINS
Community activist

URSULA JUDKINS VIEWPOINT
2605 W. GALER ST.

JULIA LEE KNUDSEN
arts volunteer

JULIA LEE'S PARK
2701 E. HARRISON ST.

AMY YEE
Tennis player and teacher

AMY YEE TENNIS CENTER
2000 MARTIN LUTHER KING JR. WAY S.

SEATTLE WOMEN!

RUBY CHOW
Restaurateur and politician

RUBY CHOW PARK
1136 S. ALBRO PL.

NORA WOODS
Community activist

NORA'S WOODS
720 29TH AVE.

MYRTLE EDWARDS
Politician

MYRTLE EDWARDS PARK
3130 ALASKAN WAY

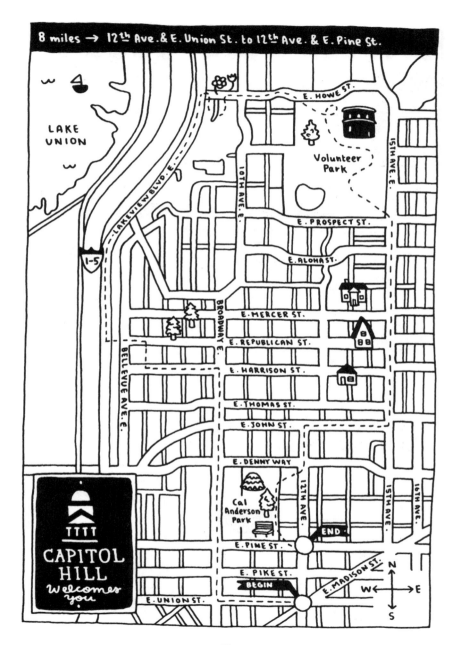

COFFEE SHOPS: ~~HHH~~ ~~HHH~~ |||

PEOPLE IN CONSTRUCTION VESTS: ~~HHH~~ ~~HHH~~ ~~HHH~~ ~~HHH~~ ~~HHH~~ ~~HHH~~

FOUND:

A cordless phone, gently used.

SHOES ON WIRES!!

E. UNION ST. BETWEEN 10TH AVE. & 11TH AVE.

E. PIKE ST. & 11TH AVE.

THE SCENE ON

E PIKE ST

one person riding a bicycle built for two

YOU GOT THIS!

a tiny breeze

ketchup packet
↓

14

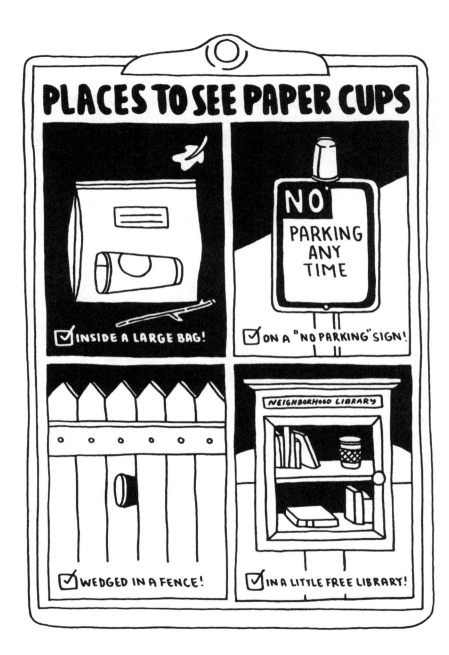

HIDDEN GEMS

MY FAVORITE TUCKED-AWAY TREASURES FROM THIS CAPITOL HILL WALK

① The Republican St. Stairs
E. Republican St. between Melrose Ave. E. & Bellevue Ave. E.

This is a beautiful and often-overlooked stairway. It's fun to walk down it and imagine what Seattle looked like when it was built.

② Streissguth Gardens
1640 Broadway E.

During my walk through here, I found a shiny pink Easter egg under a bush. It contained rainwater and one pine needle.

③ Louisa Boren Lookout
1606 15th Ave. E.

THERE'S NOTHING *BOREN* ABOUT IT!

I really love the view from this quiet spot.

CRANES SEEN FROM THE TOP OF THE WATER TOWER IN VOLUNTEER PARK: ~~JHH~~ II

BABY DUCKS IN POND: ~~JHH~~ III

OH YEAH!

Overheard on Broadway:

They may try, but they'll never take my eyeballs.

Stickers on Fire Hydrants

I did a survey of **30** Capitol Hill fire hydrants and found that there was an average of **7** street-art stickers per hydrant.

STICKIN' IT TO THE MAN!

The Seattle Daily Crier

SCANDAL IN SEATTLE!

A GREYHOUND IS SPOTTED ON THE TENNIS COURT AT CAPITOL HILL'S VOLUNTEER PARK... RIGHT NEXT TO A SIGN THAT CLEARLY STATES "NO DOGS ALLOWED"!

NO DOGS ALLOWED

NO SKATING

Seattle, WA – Despite multiple signs warning against it, a local greyhound was seen hanging out on the tennis court at Volunteer Park around 11:00 AM on Tuesday.

"He didn't seem to be an amateur tennis player," noted concerned resident

SECRET-KEEPING SIDEWALK ALLIGATOR

Hiding in plain sight on Capitol Hill is E. Union's SECRET-KEEPING SIDEWALK ALLIGATOR.

Drawn into the cement between 11th Ave. and 12th Ave., this rare reptile is eager to hear your deepest secrets. Once you've found him, crouch down really low and whisper a secret you thought you'd take to the grave... then watch in awe as he doesn't tell a soul!

PSST... I've never seen a single episode of "Doctor Who"... Please don't tell anyone...

18

The Cal Anderson Park Countdown

☑ 3 TEENAGERS JUMPING UP AND DOWN!

☑ 2 DOGS THAT LOOK LIKE BEARS!

☑ 1 SPILLED BAG OF LICORICE ALLSORTS!

CAPITOL HILL TRASH TIME!

Capitol Hill has the best sidewalk trash in Seattle, and no one can tell me otherwise!

NOTICE
Containers must be placed on hand level order

⚠ CAUTION
⊘

On this walk I saw four buttons, a pile of Christmas lights, a hanger, a dinosaur-shaped fruit snack, a broken plate, a coupon for 20% off a noninvasive face-lift, a stamp pad, and a bag of rhinestones.

TIMELINE OF SEATTLE'S
TALLEST
BUILDINGS

King Street Station
247 feet tall

Alaska Building
203 feet tall

Pioneer Building
92 feet tall

1892–1904

1904–1906

1906–1914

☆ The Space Needle is not included because it is an observation tower, not a building. However, at 605 feet, it was the tallest structure in Seattle from its completion in 1961 until 1969.

Columbia Center
933 feet tall

Safeco Plaza
630 feet tall

Smith Tower
462 feet tall

1914 - 1969

1969 - 1985

1985 - present

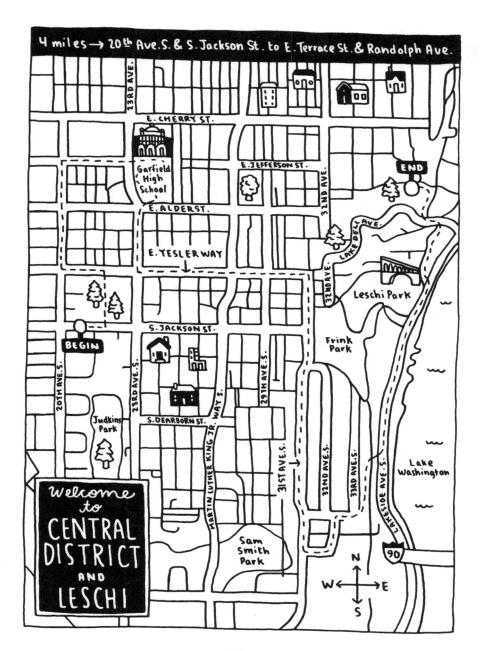

23

PLASTIC UTENSILS ON
SIDEWALK: ꟷꟷꟷ || (7)

Sidewalk Snacks

Six-and-a-half chocolate-
covered pretzels!

SIGNS FOR YARD SALES:
ꟷꟷꟷ ꟷꟷꟷ ꟷꟷꟷ

Ernestine Anderson Wy

In 2016, Seattle City Council declared S. Jackson St. from 20th Ave. S. to 23rd Ave. S. "Ernestine Anderson Way" in honor of famous jazz and blues singer and former Central District resident Ernestine Anderson (1928 - 2016), who attended Garfield High School in the 1940s.

CUTE LITTLE FREE LIBRARY

HELLO. THIS
IS A FREE
LIBRARY!
TAKE A
BOOK OR
LEAVE A
BOOK. ENJOY!

WOODEN-SPOON
HANDLE!

Top Dog! Spotted on E. Jefferson St.

HIGHLIGHTS FROM THIS WALK

LOOKING UP CAN REVEAL NEAT STUFF, LIKE GARFIELD HIGH SCHOOL'S TERRA-COTTA!

A BUS SHELTER WITH AN ABANDONED OTTOMAN INSTEAD OF A BENCH!

AN OLD STREET SIGN ON A POLE AT LAKE WASHINGTON BLVD. AND E. YESLER WAY!

A BIRDHOUSE ON TOP OF A TRAFFIC CONE!

A MISSPELLING OF "YESLER" ON THE SIDEWALK! TO ERR IS HUMAN!

25

24ᵗʰ Ave. & E. Yesler Way

A Safeway basket with one clog inside

SAFEWAY

31ˢᵗ Ave. & E. Yesler Way

THE OTHER CLOG!

The Old Leschi Trolley Bridge

Located where E. Yesler meets Lake Washington Blvd. near the entrance to Leschi Park, this former cable car bridge is a humble reminder of Seattle's transportation past. The Yesler Way trolley line connected Leschi to Pioneer Square from 1887 until 1940 and was one of Seattle's most popular routes, especially during the summer, when people would picnic on Lake Washington.

TWO NEW POINTS OF VIEW

The Leschi-Lake Dell Natural Area at 3525 E. Terrace St. is a hidden gem with a great view of Mount Rainier on a clear day.

The Mount Baker Ridge Viewpoint at 1403 31st Ave. S. gives you a unique angle on Downtown Seattle and buildings like Smith Tower and Beacon Hill's Pacific Tower.

REMINDERS OF THE 1909 ALASKA-YUKON-PACIFIC EXPO ON THE UW CAMPUS

The University of Washington campus is home to some neat Seattle history, and not just because 1936 graduate W. Ronald Benson went on to invent yellow highway paint! The campus was built on the grounds of 1909's Alaska-Yukon-Pacific (A-Y-P) Exposition, Seattle's first world's fair. Several buildings and statues built for the A-Y-P Expo remain to this day.

Architecture Hall ↗

Cunningham Hall →

Lorado Taft's George Washington statue →

Off-Campus Honorable Mention

Richard E. Brooks's William Henry Seward statue, now located in Volunteer Park ↘

31

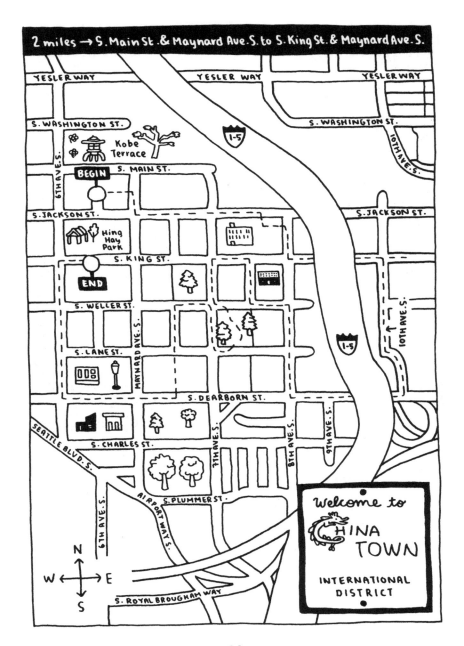

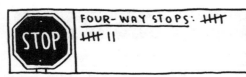 FOUR-WAY STOPS: ̶H̶H̶T̶ ̶H̶H̶T̶ II

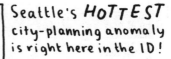 Seattle's *HOTTEST* city-planning anomaly is right here in the ID!

 FLATTENED CARDBOARD BOXES: ̶H̶H̶T̶ ̶H̶H̶T̶ ̶H̶H̶T̶ ̶H̶H̶T̶ ̶H̶H̶T̶ ̶H̶H̶T̶ ̶H̶H̶T̶ IIII

(There's no 11th Ave. S. here!)

TWO BLOCKS FOR THE PRICE OF ONE!

LOST SOCKS
of Chinatown-International District

FOUND
6th & Main

HAVE YOU SEEN ME?
Last seen outside bank

REWARD!
- baby sock
- striped
7th Ave. S.

LOST
Responds to "Ed"

MISSING
5th & Dearborn

UNBELIEVABLE!

A plastic baggie containing other, smaller plastic baggies!

SPOTTED! at Donnie Chin International Children's Park: A DOG USING A HUMAN DRINKING FOUNTAIN!!!

THIS IS THE BEST THING I HAVE EVER SEEN IN MY LIFE!

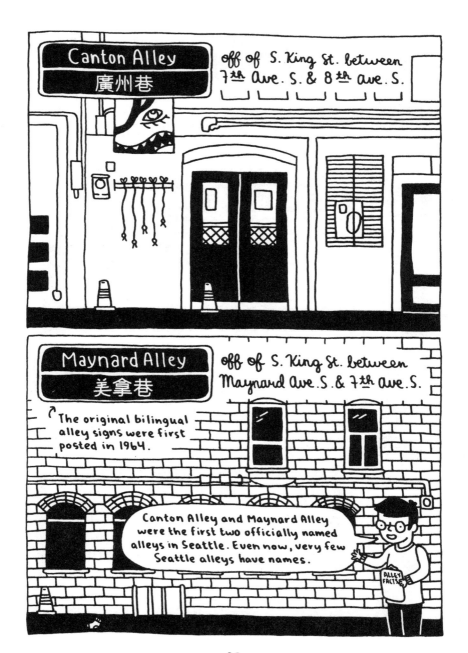

THE CHINATOWN GATE

LET'S DO THE MATH!

Construction-worker breakdown for the creation of the Chinatown Gate (according to a 2008 interview in "Northwest Asian Weekly" with architect Paul Wu):

FULL-TIMERS: 6
PART-TIMERS: 2
HOURS A DAY: 9
DAYS A WEEK: 6
MONTHS: 5

Assuming that the part-timers worked half days, the gate took 7,560 man-hours to construct!

THAT'S HOW LONG IT WOULD TAKE TO WATCH THE 1993 CLASSIC "SLEEPLESS IN SEATTLE" 4,320 TIMES!!!

HOTEL SIGNS

ALPS HOTEL

BUSH HOTEL

PANAMA HOTEL

The Panama Hotel and Tea House at 605 S. Main St. is Seattle's only NATIONAL TREASURE, a designation given in 2015 by the National Trust for Historic Preservation. The 1910 hotel was lauded for its significance to the Japanese American community, and it has preserved personal items left behind during the internment of Japanese Americans in World War II, which customers can view through a clear panel in the Tea House floor.

THE SEATTLE MUSEUM OF ALMOST OBSOLESCENCE

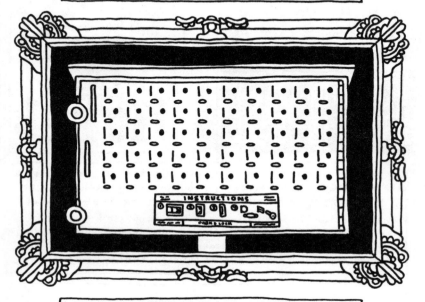

THE PARKING LOT HONOR PAY BOX
Artist Unknown

Curator statement: As carrying cash has become less common, so too have these metal parking lot pay boxes. However, you can still find them at a few of the city's parking lots, like this one on S. Lane St. and 6th Ave. S.

FIVE MINUTES ON THE CORNER OF 8TH AVE. S. & S. KING ST.

A PHONE BOOK

A SHIRT HANGING IN A WINDOW

A GUY WEARING GLASSES AND SUNGLASSES, LOOKING AT A MAP

A SQUASHED PAPER AIRPLANE

BAGS OF FORTUNE COOKIE REJECTS FOR SALE

NUMBER OF CARS THAT DROVE BY

He thinks I'm a tree and he can shake me to get money. Anyway, I'll be meeting him at the QFC later.

OVERHEARD

ARCHITECTURAL REMNANTS

BURKE
BUILDING
ARCH
915 2nd Ave.

PLYMOUTH
PILLARS
1050 Pike St.

GROUP HEALTH* TERRA-COTTA
201 16th Ave. E.

HOLLYWOOD VIDEO SIGN {BUT WHY?!} 127 Broadway E.
*Now Kaiser Permanente

HOLLYWOOD LOFTS

PEOPLE WITH SUITCASES:
~~HHT HHT HHT~~ III

PETITIONERS: ~~HHT HHT~~ I

EXCITING sighting:

A BALLOON ANIMAL!

The Central Library

 There were ˙THREE˙ people washing the windows!

The Seattle Public Library's Central Library is made up of 9,994 pieces of exterior glass!

GLASS EXPERT

44

BUILDING COURT

with the Honorable Judge Seattle Walk Report

THE DEFENDANT: The King County Administration Building, 500 4th Ave.

THE CRIME:
- "dubious aesthetics" ("The Seattle Times," 2006)
- having "the appearance of a waffle iron ("The Seattle Times," 1971)
- "I think everybody acknowledges it may be the ugliest building in downtown Seattle." – former deputy mayor Tim Ceis, 2006

EXHIBIT A

EXHIBIT B

THE VERDICT:
NOT GUILTY!

I think it looks like a sassy, box-shaped honeycomb!

SEATTLE BUILDING COURT

Pike Place Market

PEOPLE TAKING SELFIES IN FRONT OF THE MARKET SIGN: |||| |||| |||| |

PEOPLE TRYING TO DRIVE THROUGH PIKE PLACE: |||| ||

FAUX PAS!

OVERHEARD: "WHERE ARE THE T-SHIRTS?!"

GUM WALL POSES

Since the early '90s, people have been sticking gum to the walls of Post Alley under Pike Place Market and striking one of three poses for their commemorative photos:

"The Richard Nixon"

"The Pretend Like You're Eating It"

"The My Hair Just Got Stuck"

Pike Place Market sees over *10 MILLION* visitors a year, making it Seattle's most visited attraction!

10 MILLION?! That's the entire population of Sweden, as of 2019!

The Arrows of Pike Place

LOWER FLOOR

MORE SHOPS

OPEN

GAS
G

ONE WAY

RESTROOMS

← Pike Pl

LINE STARTS HERE

THE WONDERFUL WORLD OF
STANDPIPES!

Once you start noticing the dizzying array of standpipe styles on buildings around Seattle, *NOTHING IN YOUR LIFE WILL EVER BE THE SAME!*

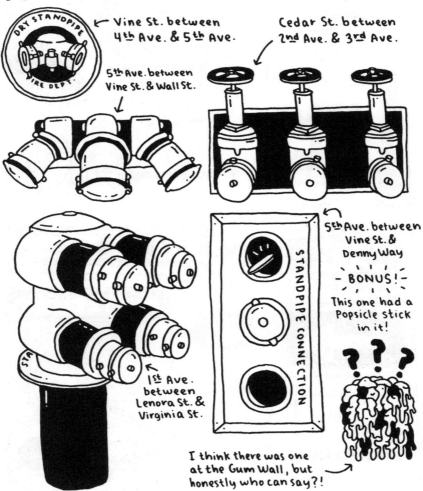

DRY STANDPIPE · FIRE DEPT.

← Vine St. between 4ᵗʰ Ave. & 5ᵗʰ Ave.

Cedar St. between 2ⁿᵈ Ave. & 3ʳᵈ Ave.

5ᵗʰ Ave. between Vine St. & Wall St.

STANDPIPE CONNECTION

5ᵗʰ Ave. between Vine St. & Denny Way

- BONUS! -
This one had a Popsicle stick in it!

1ˢᵗ Ave. between Lenora St. & Virginia St.

? ? ?

I think there was one at the Gum Wall, but honestly who can say?!

SIGHTS OF THE SOUND
on the Waterfront

A PRESSED-PENNY MACHINE

A CHILD WITH A GIANT LOLLIPOP, CRYING BECAUSE HIS MOM SAID THAT HE IS TOO YOUNG TO OPERATE A FERRY

A CUTE DOG NAPPING NEAR WATERFRONT PARK

★SEATTLE BRIDGES

ARBORETUM AQUEDUCT, 1911

Designed by the same architect as Queen Anne's Willcox Wall (see page 107)!

FREMONT BRIDGE, 1917

Over one million bicyclists crossed the Fremont Bridge in 2018!

MAGNOLIA BRIDGE, 1930

Originally named the Garfield Street Bridge. Where's the lasagna?!

WORTH WALKING ★

AURORA BRIDGE, 1932 — This bridge was dedicated on George Washington's 200th birthday!

COWEN PARK BRIDGE, 1936 — An art deco gem!

SOUTH PARK BRIDGE, 2014 — This bridge has 750,000 feet of electrical wiring!

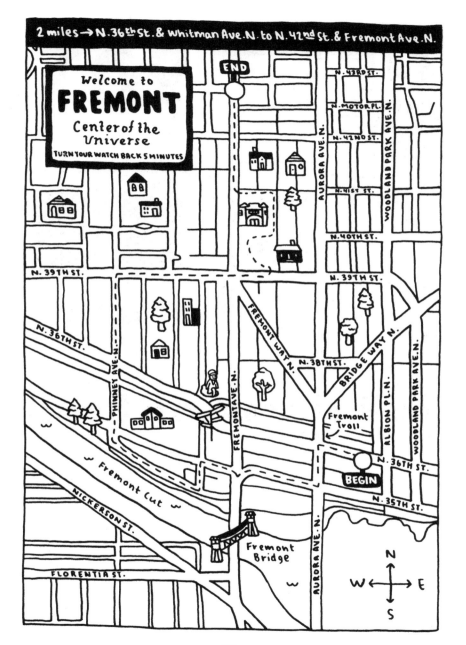

PEOPLE LOOKING AT THE FREMONT TROLL: ЖІ III

STARBUCKS CUPS: ЖІ ЖІ

Caught in the act!

A DAYTIME RACCOON!

FOUND: a winning scratch-off ticket!

WALKING PAYS! I always pick up the scratch-off tickets I find on the ground while out walking, but I've never found a winner until now! I'm $5 richer!

$1
APPLE BUCK$
$5 $5
$1 $5 $1
Win up to $5,000!

Yarn-bombed tree

The Real Dinosaurs of Fremont

APATOSAURUS TOPIARIES ON N. CANAL ST.!

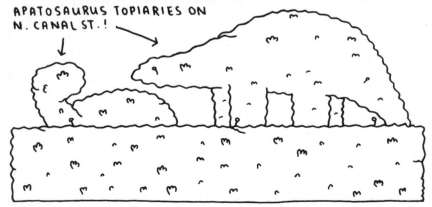

TOWERING TREASURES

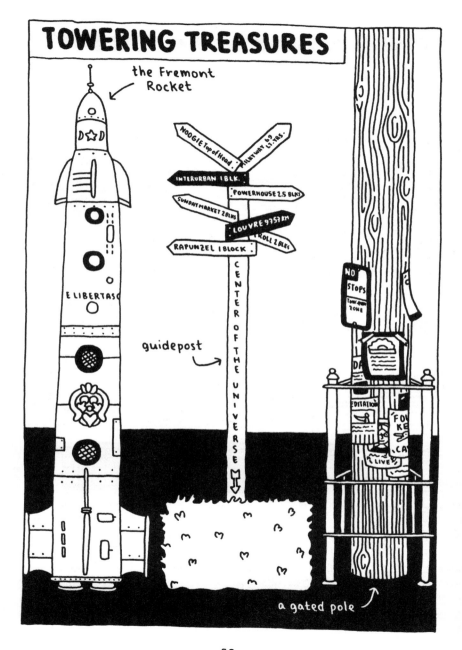

the Fremont Rocket

D☆D

E LIBERTAS

guidepost

NOOGIE Top of Head

MILKY WAY 6.9 LT.YRS.

INTERURBAN 1 BLK.

POWERHOUSE 2.5 BLKS

SUNDAY MARKET 2 BLKS

LOUVRE 9757 KM

TROLL 2 BLKS

RAPUNZEL 1 BLOCK

CENTER OF THE UNIVERSE

NO STOPS
TOW AWAY ZONE

MEDITATION

FOU KE CAT

LIVE

a gated pole

The Fremont Trolley Barn

on Phinney Ave. S. was formerly home to Redhook Ale Brewery and is now the Theo Chocolate factory.

B.F. Day Elementary

on Linden Ave. N. has been open since 1892, making it the Seattle School District's oldest continually operating school!

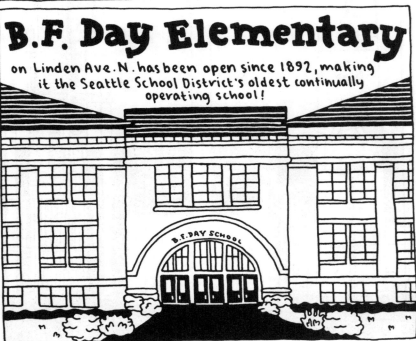

It's time for Seattle's **FAVORITE** game show...

TRASH OR GUERILLA ART INSTALLATION?

FREMONT EDITION!

The game show where YOU decide if outdoor finds are misunderstood pieces of public art or if they're just regular ol' garbage!

CONTESTANT 1	**CONTESTANT 2**	**CONTESTANT 3**
Four Amazon boxes stacked like a cairn on N. 38th St.	A lone saltine next to a totally sealed box of saltines on Fremont Way N.	A lamp surrounded by peanut shells on Linden Ave. N.

☐ TRASH!
☐ GUERILLA ART INSTALLATION!

☐ TRASH!
☐ GUERILLA ART INSTALLATION!

☐ TRASH!
☐ GUERILLA ART INSTALLATION!

57

People of Fremont

A KID USING THEIR FACE TO PRESS A CROSSWALK BUTTON

TWO PEOPLE HOLDING HANDS EVEN THOUGH IT IS CURRENTLY INCONVENIENT TO DO SO

SOMEONE WEARING A THROWING DISC AS A NECKLACE

A CHILD WHO HAS WATCHED TOO MUCH "LAW & ORDER"

Yeah, but your eyes tell a different story...

Notable Finds from the Fremont Sunday Market

← polka-dot sweatshirt

all kinds of bottles

MILK

← buttons

churros

← cute old mirror

a variety of peppers

this mug

embroidered towel

← toy snake

this scary teapot shaped like a sad dog

a dresser

← keys

cat on a leash (not for sale)

Blackberry Bushes

Blackberry bushes are such a deeply entrenched part of Seattle's landscape. They are EVERYWHERE. If you walk around the city in the late summer, you're never too far from a berry-bearing bramble. Based on their aggressive abundance, it's reasonable to think that they must be native to the Pacific Northwest.

But actually, all these things are older than the Himalayan blackberry bushes in Seattle!

← postage stamps!

dynamite!

lightbulbs!
staplers!

↖ safety pins!

cash registers!

𝒟 ←jelly beans!

Morse code! ↴
.... .. / -.. .- -.. .-.- --

bicycles! ↝

←paper bags!

⌇ feather dusters!

The blackberries we know today didn't appear here until <u>1885</u>!
How did this invasive species come so far, so fast?

Luther Burbank was a

LUTHER BURBANK
PLANT WIZARD
1849-1926

botanist and horticulturalist interested in plant breeding. Burbank created many megahits that we still enjoy today:

elephant garlic!

russet Burbank potatoes!

Shasta daisies!

the plumcot!

fire poppies!

And some less popular plants that we don't:

a potato-tomato hybrid!

HELP!

a plum called "Geewhiz"!

walnuts with a paper-like shell!

In addition to concocting his own creations, Burbank also participated in seed exchanges and imported seeds from around the world. During one such exchange, he received blackberry seeds. Dubbing them the "Himalayan Giant," he noted from his Santa Rosa home that they grew vigorously and abundantly: the perfect backyard plant!

The seeds were distributed through his seed catalogs at first, and then nature took its course, with birds and animals spreading the seeds far and wide. It just so happened that the climate of the Pacific Northwest, combined with the ease with which these plants could reproduce, created the perfect opportunity for the kind of blackberry behemoths we see today, and thus, a Seattle landscape legend was born!

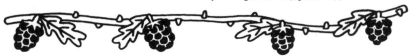

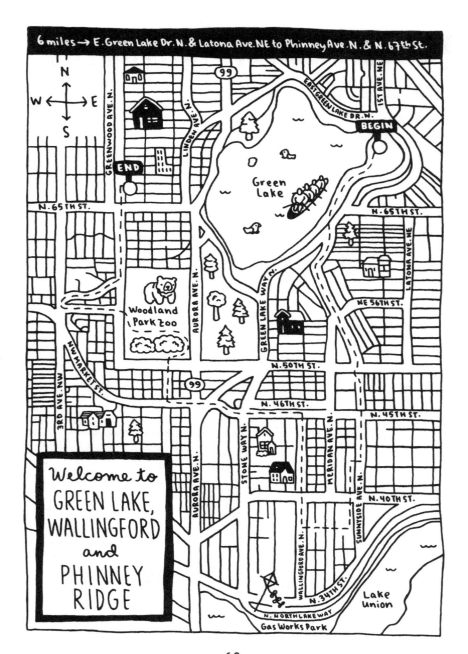

SPIDERWEBS: 卌 卌 卌 卌 卌 |||

CANDY WRAPPERS: 卌 卌 |

← wild-rabbit sighting near Green Lake!

MYSTERIOUS DISCOVERY:

a Dunkin' Donuts coffee cup... and the closest Dunkin' Donuts is more than 800 miles away!

Charming Building Alert!
The Good Shepherd Center on Sunnyside Ave. N.

THE DOGS OF GREEN LAKE

According to the 2010 census and Seattle Animal Shelter data, dogs outnumber children in Seattle. This is very apparent at Green Lake.

Fire Hydrant Styles
of Phinney Ridge

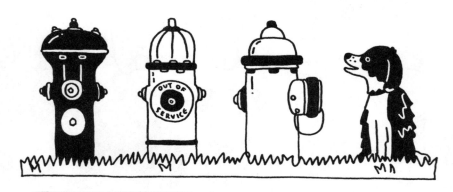

DESIRE PATHS

A desire path is formed when repeated foot traffic causes the ground to erode, creating a path of pedestrian consensus rather than the designated path. Often, it's the shortest route between two points.

Desire paths can be seen (and walked!) everywhere, but it's especially fun to be on the lookout for them at a place like Green Lake, where so many people walk and run.

Here are two desire paths spotted at Green Lake:

Around some large trees off of E. Green Lake Dr. N.

By the Green Lake Park Wading Pool (could this be a stroller desire path?)

Things in the Woodland Park Rose Garden other than Roses

a stone bench

some lumpy topiaries →

a baby carrot

← a QFC receipt

QFC

← lily pads

← tall grass

a bee

grouchy lion terra-cotta by the reflecting pool

← a gazebo

SKY SPOTTING

A SEAPLANE!

A FANCY KITE!

A CLOUD SHAPED LIKE A CUTE TURTLE!

BIRDS DOING THEIR BIRD THING!

DRINKING FOUNTAIN POP QUIZ

How well do you know Seattle's public drinking fountains? Test your knowledge and impress your friends!

According to Seattle Parks and Recreation data from 2018...

① How many outdoor public drinking fountains does Seattle have?

    A. 111

    B. 211

    C. 311

② Which one of these parks has the MOST outdoor public drinking fountains?

    A. Discovery Park

    B. Seward Park

    C. Woodland Park

③ Which one of these neighborhoods has NO outdoor public drinking fountains?

    A. Wedgwood

    B. Columbia City

    C. Alki

☆ Answers on page 157!

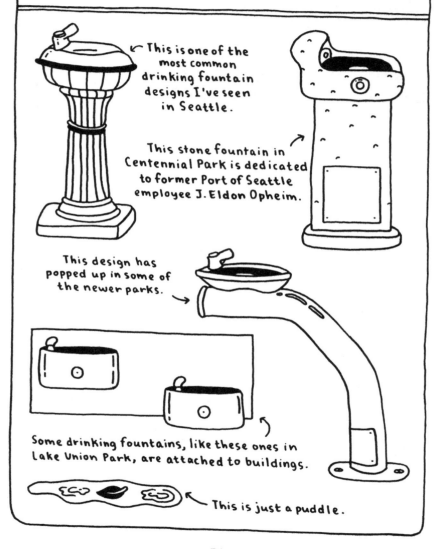

This is one of the most common drinking fountain designs I've seen in Seattle.

This stone fountain in Centennial Park is dedicated to former Port of Seattle employee J. Eldon Opheim.

This design has popped up in some of the newer parks.

Some drinking fountains, like these ones in Lake Union Park, are attached to buildings.

This is just a puddle.

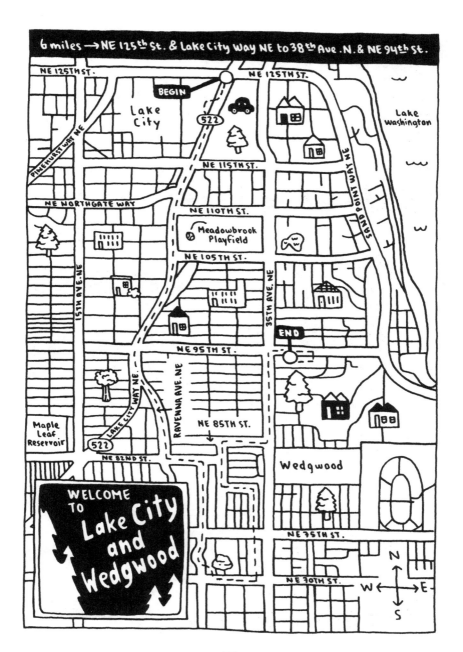

TINY APPLES: ||||| |||||
||||| ||||| ||

 CROSSWALKS THAT MADE
ME WAIT: ||||| ||||| |||||

FOUND: a sandless
turtle-shaped sandbox

I'M SO EMPTY INSIDE!

Wedgwood Window Dogs

Totally enchanting: this oval-shaped roundabout
on Hiram Pl. NE!

LAKE CITY & WEDGWOOD HIGHLIGHTS

FORMER SEAFIRST BANK ENTRANCE ON LAKE CITY WAY

THE WEDGWOOD ROCK

A FREE TREE...

FREE

...IN AUGUST!

CUTE RED VW BUG

DESERTED FLANNEL SHIRT

A TACO-SHAPED BALLOON

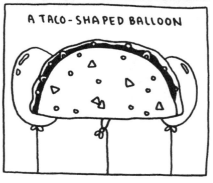

Let's take a moment to appreciate the tops of these metal gates in Wedgwood!

Seattle Walk Report is
Bad at Birdwatching

Proud high school graduate and budding ornithologist Seattle Walk Report shares some of her favorite winged wonders in Lake City and Wedgwood.

NAME: The Flim-Flam Fluttress
HABITAT: Lake City Way used car lots
FEEDING: Leftover lettuce from Dick's Drive-In
OTHER NOTES: Enjoys true-crime podcasts and learning to live with regret

NAME: The Beady-Eyed Babeldon
HABITAT: Near Eckstein Middle School
FEEDING: A nonstop onion-rings party
OTHER NOTES: His great uncle made a brief appearance in 1987's "Harry and the Hendersons"

NAME: The North American Winged Woopie
HABITAT: Wedgwood's Penguin Park
FEEDING: Your family's picnic
OTHER NOTES: Has shrill voice that frequently complains about traffic

CAH! CAH! Isn't it time for another salmon truck to tip over? I'm hungry!

What's Growing on in the Picardo Farm P-Patch?

The Picardo Farm P-Patch in Wedgwood was Seattle's first official community garden. In fact, the "P" in "P-Patch" stands for "Picardo"!

lots of cherry tomatoes

plums

dahlias

great gourds

a droopy sunflower

a mystery plant

chard

quinoa

zucchinis

tomatoes

eggplants

radishes

green onions

DISTINGUISHED

ELEPHANT CAR WASH SIGN: 616 Battery St.

This pink icon has been lighting up Denny Way since 1956!

<u>Height of an adult African elephant</u>: 10-13 feet at the shoulder

<u>Height of the Elephant Car Wash sign</u>: 18 feet

If you stacked 34 of these signs on top of each other, they would reach the top of the Space Needle! I don't know why you would do that, but to each their own.

ELEPHANTS!

THE AURORA ELEPHANT : 8800 Aurora Ave. N.

After being built in Fremont during the 1930s, this elephant made the move to Aurora Ave. N. in 1946 and has been gracing us with its steady presence ever since.

Weight of an adult African elephant: Nearly 18,000 pounds

Weight of the Aurora Elephant: 9,500 pounds

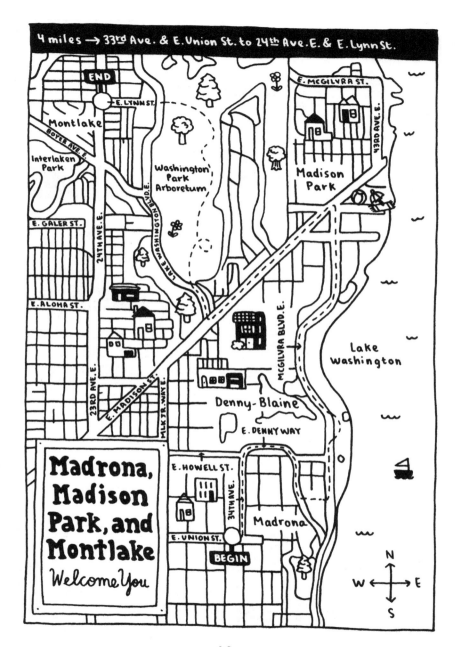

PEOPLE WITH STROLLERS:
~~HHH HHH HHH~~ IIII

BICYCLISTS ON LAKE WASHINGTON BLVD.:
~~HHH HHH HHH HHH~~ I

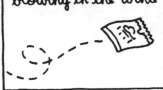

Spotted: a Dick's french fry wrapper blowing in the wind

LITTLE FREE LIBRARY ALERT!

- OH WAIT! - IT'S THE MADRONA-SALLY GOLDMARK BRANCH!

1,707 SQUARE FEET!

What's on the Kurt Cobain Bench?

This bench in Viretta Park on Lake Washington Blvd. E. serves as an unofficial memorial for Nirvana's Kurt Cobain.

two empty beer cans — a notepad — several candles
a ladybug
about $1.50 in change
a friendship bracelet — flowers — a broken phone

A DOG WALKER!

Spotted on E. Lynn St.

Three Things Seen During Three Minutes on E. Denny Way

Adorable bus stop

Epiphany Parish

SO MANY DUCKS in Denny Blaine Lake Park

Lake Washington Blvd.
is on the National Register of Historic Places!

There is a Lake Washington Blvd. E....

Lk Washington Blvd E

...and an E. Lake Washington Blvd.!

E Lk Washington Blvd

Most street signs in Seattle are green, but some, like those along Lake Washington Blvd., are brown! Brown street signs indicate one of three things: Parks Department roads, honorary street names, or Olmsted boulevards. Lake Washington is an Olmsted boulevard, named for the Olmsted Brothers landscape architecture firm, which made a series of recommendations for bolstering Seattle's parks and boulevards in the early 20th century.

NEAT FIND! The Pine St. pedestrian bridge is a wooden walkway that takes you over a ravine between Grand Ave. and Madrona Dr.!

I WOOD walk over this bridge again!

SO YOU'VE BEEN ATTACKED BY A CROW IN MONTLAKE!

I've been attacked by crows three times in my life, and all three times have been in the Montlake area! Be careful walking through here during the spring and summer, when crows are trying to defend their territory and their young.

To protect yourself from crow attacks, the Washington Department of Fish and Wildlife recommends the following:

SLOWLY WAVING YOUR ARMS OVERHEAD!

WEARING A HAT OR HELMET!

CARRYING AN UMBRELLA!

TRY ALL 3!

Valentines

to My Favorite Plants in the Arboretum

My love for you grows abundantly, like a rhododendron bush.

YOU'RE JUST LIKE SCOLOPENDRIFOLIUM...

Hard to read. ♡

Are you witch hazel?

Because you've cast a spell on me.

I'm *PINING* for you!

SEATTLE'S GLACIAL LAKES

I miss the old Seattle! Like, remember the good ol' days of about 13,000 years ago, when a sheet of ice was slowly sliding from what is now British Columbia into the Puget Sound region? **_UGH_**! Seattle transplants just don't get it. The city has changed, man.

This all happened during the Vashon Glaciation, when the giant glacier covering the region began to melt. The ice sheet was known as the Cordilleran Ice Sheet, and we have the aftermath of its travels to thank for forming many of the lakes we enjoy today. The next time you're taking a selfie in front of one of these bodies of water, whisper a little "thank you" to the Cordilleran Ice Sheet! Stay cool.

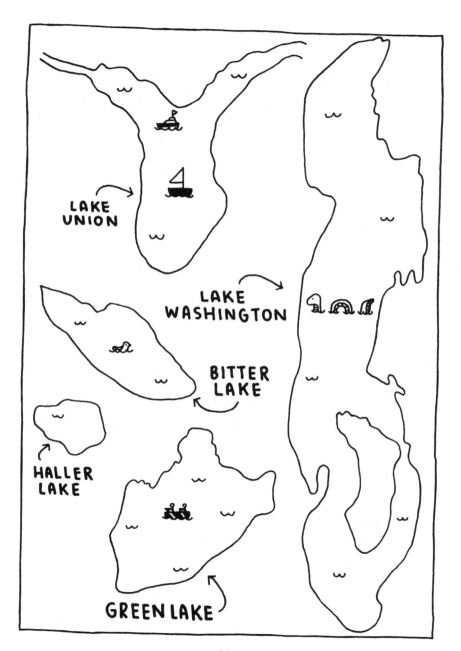

LAKE
UNION

LAKE
WASHINGTON

BITTER
LAKE

HALLER
LAKE

GREEN LAKE

Pioneer Square

Pioneer Square is the place to go if you enjoy cool old buildings. I like walking around here and thinking about all the people and places that have called Pioneer Square home over its long history. It's also very flat and easy to navigate, making it a great choice for a short walk.

If you walk here, be on the lookout for:
- ☑ ghost signs (old, hand-painted signs on the sides of buildings)
- ☑ art galleries
- ☑ pigeons on the hunt for food
- ☑ neat architecture

GOLD BARS

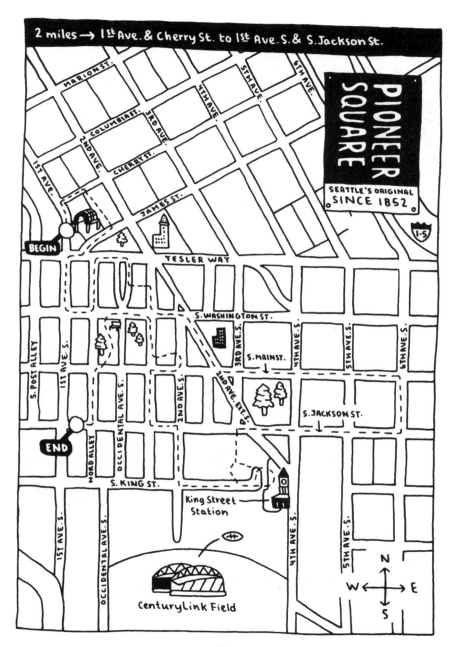

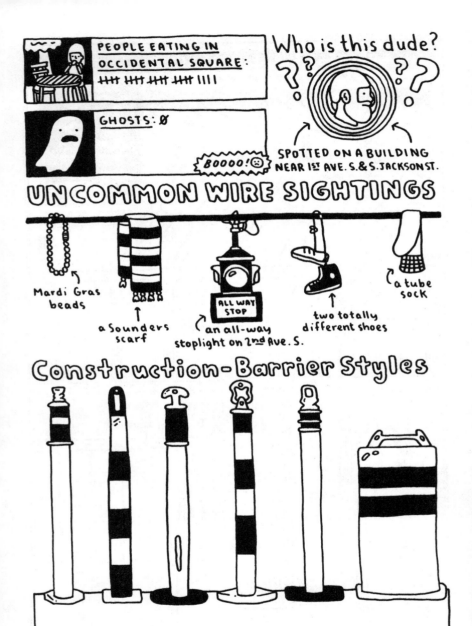

PEOPLE EATING IN OCCIDENTAL SQUARE: ⲦⲎⲦ ⲦⲎⲦ ⲦⲎⲦ ⲦⲎⲦ IIII

GHOSTS: Ø

BOOOO! ☹

Who is this dude?

??? ? ? ?

SPOTTED ON A BUILDING NEAR 1ST AVE. S. & S. JACKSON ST.

UNCOMMON WIRE SIGHTINGS

Mardi Gras beads

a Sounders scarf

ALL WAY STOP

an all-way stoplight on 2nd Ave. S.

two totally different shoes

a tube sock

Construction-Barrier Styles

THE GREATEST EVENT IN ALL SEATTLE HISTORY

→ IT'S THE MATCH OF THE CENTURY! ←

See it LIVE **Pioneer Square SHOWDOWN!**

TUE. JULY 5TH

DID I COUNT MORE **PIGEONS** OR ART **GALLERIES?**

<u>NO</u> RULES
<u>NO</u> LIMITS
<u>NO</u> DUCKS

PIGEON COUNT:
~~||||~~ ~~||||~~ ~~||||~~ ~~||||~~

ART GALLERY COUNT:
~~||||~~ ~~||||~~ ~~||||~~ |

PIGEONS WIN... THIS TIME!

DIRECT FROM PIONEER SQUARE • SEATTLE, WA, USA

95

PLACES I SAW CAUTION TAPE

TIED AROUND A TREE!

ON A POTTED PLANT!

IN A DOORWAY!

HANGING OFF A SIGN!

WATERFALL GARDEN PARK

This park opened in 1978 on the site of the first UPS headquarters.

IRON PERGOLA & TOTEM POLE

The iron pergola was built in 1909 as a stop for the Yesler and James Street Cable Car Company.

In 1899, a totem pole was stolen from a Tlingit village in Alaska and brought to Pioneer Square. After an arsonist burned it down in 1938, this reproduction pole replaced it in 1940.

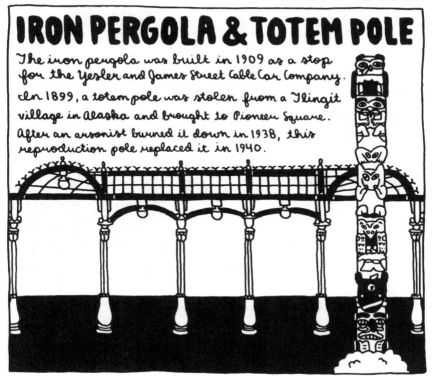

THE LIGHTS OF KING STREET STATION

HORSES of Pioneer Square

← horse head on a stick in a toy store window

← horse sculpture near 2nd Ave. S. & S. Jackson St.

← child wearing horse shirt

← giant knight in Occidental Square

98

Historic Building Entrances

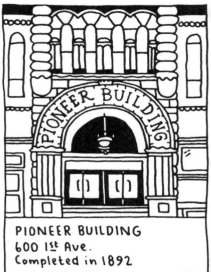

PIONEER BUILDING
600 1st Ave.
Completed in 1892

INTERURBAN BUILDING
102 Occidental Ave. S.
Completed in 1892

TERRY DENNY BUILDING
109 1st Ave.
Completed in 1891

MUTUAL LIFE BUILDING
605 1st Ave.
Completed in 1897

SEATTLE'S NEXT top rock

Hey! I'm the Wedgwood Rock. For 14,000 years I've been Seattle's top rock, and now it's time to usher in a new generation of geological delights. Who has what it takes to make it? This... is "Seattle's Next Top Rock."

NAME: The Ravenna Park Rock
LIKES: Reviewing SQL reports, project management
DISLIKES: When kids say "Thomas the Train" instead of "Thomas the Tank Engine." *HE'S A DANG TANK ENGINE!*

NAME: The Thornton Creek Rock
LIKES: Biscuits with extra butter, spending time with my grandchildren
DISLIKES: Trying to fold fitted sheets

NAME: The Leschi Park Rock

LIKES: Playing bass in my jam band, the Emerald City Erratics

DISLIKES: Haters

NAME: The rock outside of the Beacon Hill Branch Library on the Beacon Ave. S. side

LIKES: Ken Burns documentaries

DISLIKES: Loud noises

AND SEATTLE'S NEXT TOP ROCK IS...

THE ROCK OUTSIDE OF THE BEACON HILL BRANCH LIBRARY!

It looks like half of a grilled panini and has definite lasting star power.

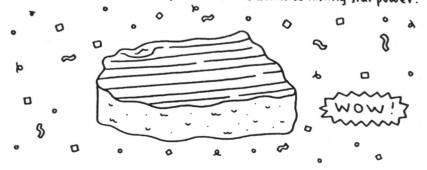

WOW!

LOWER QUEEN ANNE

Downtown's neighbor Lower Queen Anne is a lively area perfect for walking. Look for mid-century architecture, cute apartments, and great public spaces.

3 miles → Mercer St. & Dexter Ave. N. to 7th Ave. W. & W. Olympic Pl.

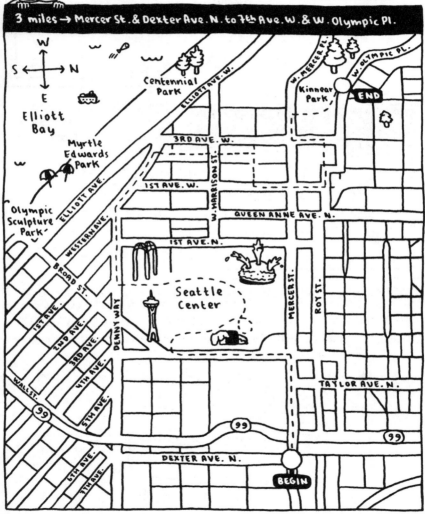

SCHOOL BUSES: ||||| ||||| |||

SNOOZING BABIES: ||||| |||

A parking meter wearing a tie!

2 HOURS MAX
PAY 8AM-8PM

cards

coins

LOOKING SHARP!

St. Paul's Episcopal Church has the best roof in Seattle!

This building has **ALL** the right angles!

DOMES & SPHERES!

Those *other* Seattle spheres can step aside! These domes and spheres are Seattle originals.

The "Seattle Post-Intelligencer" newspaper globe

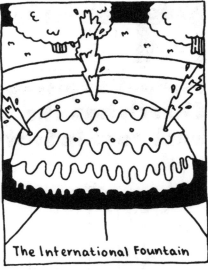

The International Fountain

Concrete balls outside of KeyArena

SPHERE OF YESTERYEAR
Gone but not forgotten!

The Bubbleator, a clear, spherical elevator that was part of the 1962 Seattle World's Fair, whose grounds became the Seattle Center!

CITY TEXTURES

in Lower Queen Anne

Concrete barrier on W. Mercer St.

Grass outside apartment building on W. Mercer St.

Siding of the Pacific Science Center in Seattle Center

Ivy on wall along Mercer St.

Terra-cotta on W. Roy St. apartment building

UPPER QUEEN ANNE

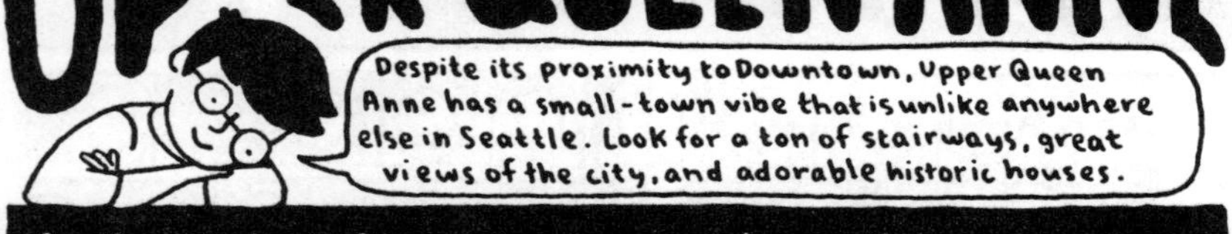

2 miles → W. Roy St. & Queen Anne Ave. N. to 3rd Ave. W. & W. Highland Dr.

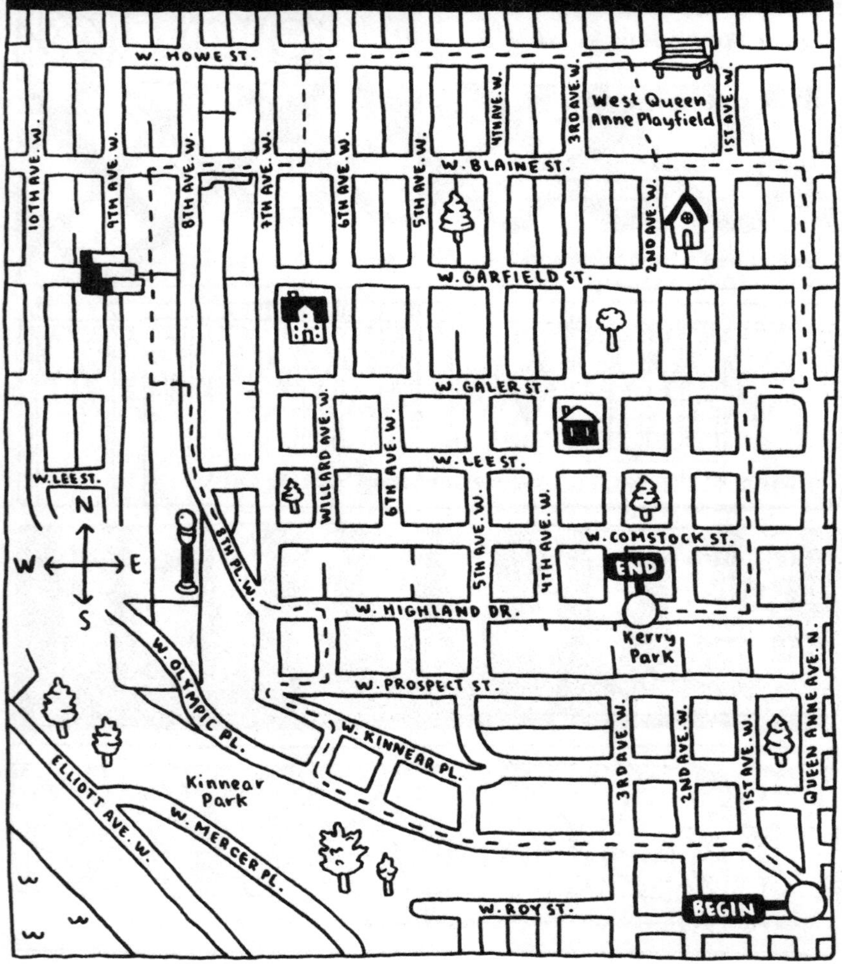

PUBLIC STAIRWAYS

Queen Anne is home to over 100 city-maintained public stairways, more than any other neighborhood in Seattle.

Here are some favorites!

This narrow pipe-rail staircase connects 8th Ave. W. and 9th Ave. W. along W. Garfield St.

The staircase on 6th Ave. W. and W. Highland Dr. is from the early 20th century!

The Willcox Wall on 8th Ave. W. is a unique and beautiful staircase from 1915.

MAGICAL APARTMENT COURTYARDS ON W. OLYMPIC PL.

De la Mar Apartments, 1909

Chelsea Apartments, 1907

LOOK AT THIS ADORABLE DOG!

This sweet old golden retriever was hanging out at a playfield.

← white face!

← little bandanna!

← perfect angel!

Queen Anne Benches

Someone left a baseball cap behind on this bench.

These two benches don't have backs on them.

← This bench seems very no-nonsense.

Children's Books

This bench comes with a bonus Little Free Library!

Seattle's
SISTER CITIES!

Seattle has 21 sister cities! Sister cities represent symbolic agreements between cities and are meant to cultivate friendship and encourage exchange, trade, and tourism.

Seattle's first sister city relationship was formed in 1957 with Kobe, Japan, and its most recent was formed in 1999 with Kâmpóng Saôm, Cambodia. Monuments and tributes celebrating Seattle's sister cities can be found throughout many neighborhoods.

KOBE, JAPAN
Trees and lantern in Kobe Terrace Park

BERGEN, NORWAY
Bergen Place Park in Ballard

DAEJEON, SOUTH KOREA

Daejeon Park in Beacon Hill

CHRISTCHURCH, NEW ZEALAND

New Zealand Focal Forest in the Arboretum

TASHKENT, UZBEKISTAN

Tashkent Park in Capitol Hill

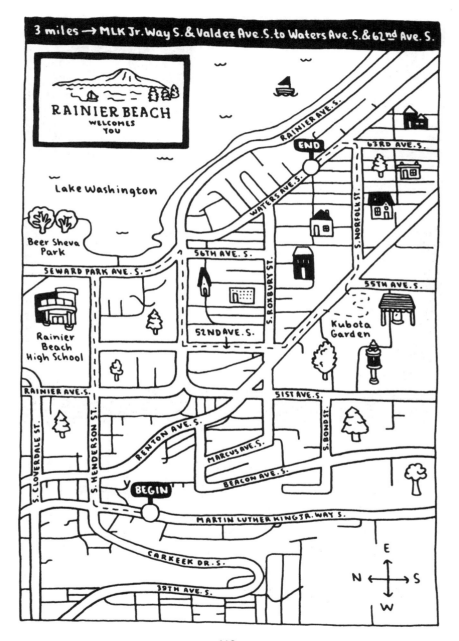

3 miles → MLK Jr. Way S. & Valdez Ave. S. to Waters Ave. S. & 62nd Ave. S.

RAINIER BEACH
WELCOMES
YOU

Lake Washington

Beer Sheva Park

Rainier Beach High School

SEWARD PARK AVE. S.

56TH AVE. S.

52ND AVE. S.

S. ROXBURY ST.

RAINIER AVE. S.

WATERS AVE. S.

END

63RD AVE. S.

S. NORFOLK ST.

55TH AVE. S.

Kubota Garden

RAINIER AVE. S.

51ST AVE. S.

S. CLOVERDALE ST.

S. HENDERSON ST.

RENTON AVE. S.

MARCUS AVE. S.

BEACON AVE. S.

S. BOND ST.

BEGIN

MARTIN LUTHER KING JR. WAY S.

CARKEEK DR. S.

39TH AVE. S.

E
N ← → S
W

PEOPLE IN SEAHAWKS GEAR: ~~IIII~~ ~~IIII~~ IIII

? ? TRAFFIC CONES THAT DON'T SEEM TO INDICATE ANYTHING: ~~IIII~~ ~~IIII~~ ~~IIII~~ III

One bulldog!

FOUND: a crisp $1 bill in a pile of leaves under a tree in Rainier Beach

WAIT A MINUTE! Is this a money tree?!

SIDEWALK FINDS

a "Wet Floor" sign

a confident duck

a hair dryer in an orange box

ORANGES

a "Dead End" sign

a tire

a toy train

DEAD END

a computer monitor

an invisible man a pile of clothes

a well-worn copy of "Eat, Pray, Love"

EAT, PRAY, LOVE

HELP METRO ROUTE 7 GET TO RAINIER BEACH!

Route 7 is one of Seattle's most popular bus routes, averaging 11,000 riders daily. Can you help the bus make its 11-mile journey to Rainier Beach? Find the answer on page 157!

START

You made a wrong turn and ended up getting lost in TUKWILA!

OH NO! A seagull boarded the bus and is making a scene!

Someone decided to eat sardines on the bus, and now it needs to be evacuated!

You got a flat tire! All the passengers are mad at you!

FINISH

RAINIER BEACH STOP

you did it!

Kubota Garden

is the most beautiful park in Seattle!

Kubota Garden was created in 1927 by gardener Fujitaro Kubota (1879-1973), who had no formal training. COOL! It has been a public park since 1987.

Rainier Beach Roundabout Tasting Notes
S. Norfolk St. Edition

① S. Norfolk St. and 61st Ave. SW
Notes: *Subtle, hint of oak*

② S. Norfolk St. and 59th Ave. SW
Notes: *Intellectually satisfying with a pleasant balance*

③ S. Norfolk St. and 57th Ave. SW
Notes: *Full-bodied, refined*

ANATOMY of a UTILITY POLE

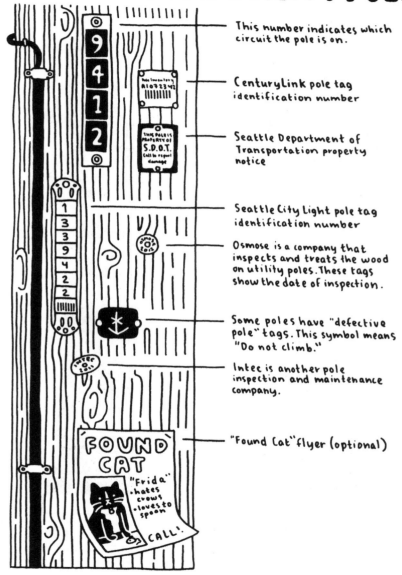

This number indicates which circuit the pole is on.

CenturyLink pole tag identification number

Seattle Department of Transportation property notice

Seattle City Light pole tag identification number

Osmose is a company that inspects and treats the wood on utility poles. These tags show the date of inspection.

Some poles have "defective pole" tags. This symbol means "Do not climb."

Intec is another pole inspection and maintenance company.

"Found Cat" flyer (optional)

Light Fixture

CARROLL'S
DIAMONDS - WATCHES

OUTSIDE MOHAI
SOUTH LAKE UNION

BY THE IRON PERGOLA
PIONEER SQUARE

Fixations

BY THE MONTLAKE BRIDGE

THROUGHOUT DOWNTOWN

SoDo & Georgetown

It may not be everyone's cup of tea, but I find that walking through the industrial areas that make up SoDo is a unique and worthwhile experience. The long stretches of solitude can make you feel like you're the only person in the city. If you enjoy a more traditional walk, Georgetown has loads of character and plenty to see on foot.

If you walk here, be on the lookout for:
- ☑ train tracks
- ☑ neon signs
- ☑ historic buildings in Georgetown
- ☑ public art
- ☑ sports fans

GO SPORTS!

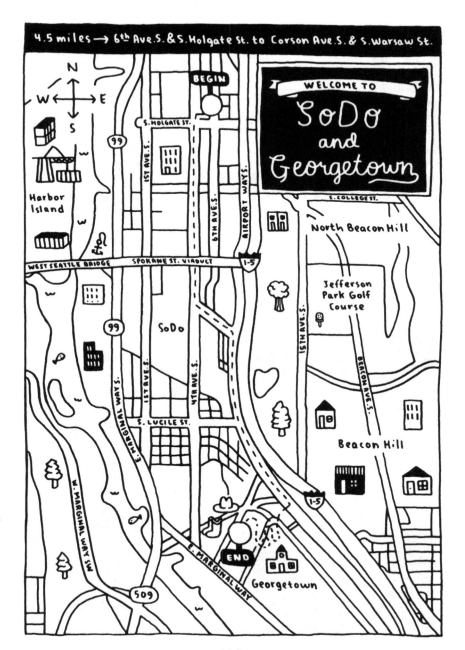

4.5 miles → 6th Ave.S. & S. Holgate St. to Corson Ave.S. & S.Warsaw St.

N
W — E
S

BEGIN

WELCOME TO
SoDo
and
Georgetown

S. HOLGATE ST.

99

1ST AVE. S.

6TH AVE. S.

AIRPORT WAY S.

S. COLLEGE ST.

Harbor Island

North Beacon Hill

WEST SEATTLE BRIDGE

SPOKANE ST. VIADUCT

I-5

Jefferson Park Golf Course

99

SoDo

1ST AVE. S.

E. MARGINAL WAY S.

1ST AVE. S.

4TH AVE. S.

BEACON AVE. S.

S. LUCILE ST.

Beacon Hill

I-5

W. MARGINAL WAY SW

E. MARGINAL WAY

END

Georgetown

509

LONESOME SHOES: ⅠⅠⅠⅠⅠ ⅠⅠⅠⅠⅠ Ⅰ

DANGER
NO
TRESPASSING

"NO TRESPASSING" SIGNS:
ⅠⅠⅠⅠⅠ ⅠⅠⅠⅠⅠ ⅠⅠⅠⅠⅠ ⅠⅠⅠⅠⅠ ⅠⅠⅠⅠⅠ ⅠⅠⅠⅠⅠ

FIRE STATION 14

at 4th Ave. S. and S. Horton St. has a cool 7-story tower built into it that has been used for firefighter training!

HOT STUFF!

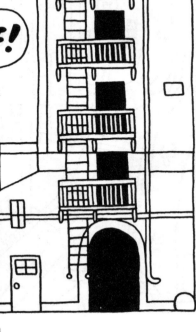

also on 4th Ave. S.:
a traffic cone with a face

AWWWW!

UNSOLVED MYSTERIES IN GEORGETOWN

A GROUND-LEVEL MAILBOX
≷ IS THIS A MAILBOX FOR DOGS?! ≷

MAIL

A MOUNTAIN DEW CAN ON A POLE RIGHT NEXT TO A RECYCLING BIN

A BLACK CAT CROSSING MY PATH

A FOAM HEAD

3 BLACK BEANIES

A NAME TAG THAT SAYS "TONY"

HELLO I'M Tony

VEHICLES in SODO

A SCHOOL BUS

A PARKING-ENFORCEMENT CART

A TRICYCLE

UNEXPECTED!

A SKATEBOARD

A SCOOTER

THE RAPIDRIDE "C" LINE

HYBRID ELECTRIC   RAPIDRIDE

The mountain is _OUT_ near Boeing Field

Not-so-fun fact: Research from the US Geological Survey found that Mount Rainier is the most threatening volcano in the Cascades and one of the most potentially dangerous volcanoes in the nation.
But it sure is pretty!

The Evolution of Georgetown City Hall

From 1904 until 1910, Georgetown was a separate city from Seattle. As such, city officials built a city hall in 1909 to house various city departments. Today the building is a treasured landmark that still serves the community.

1909: Georgetown City Hall

1925: Clinic, library & police station

The clock tower was removed over concerns that airplane vibrations from nearby Boeing Field would cause damage to the structure.

1966: Police station

Luckily, it was rebuilt!

TODAY: Dental clinic

HAT & BOOTS

The Hat and Boots were originally built in 1954 for a western-themed gas station. In 2003 they were moved to their current location in Georgetown's Oxbow Park.

CLIMBING ON HAT IS PROHIBITED VIOLATORS WILL BE CITATIONED

← My favorite thing about the Hat and Boots is this sign, both because it is very specific and because it uses the word "citationed," which I'm pretty sure doesn't exist.

129

CARNEGIE LIBRARIES

West Seattle Branch   opened 1910

Green Lake Branch   opened 1910

University Branch   opened 1910

Carnegie Libraries are libraries that were built with funds from steel tycoon, philantropist, and bearded man Andrew Carnegie. Six of the public Carnegie Libraries built in Seattle during the early part of the 20th century still maintain their original function as libraries. They are true gems of the city!

Queen Anne Branch opened 1914

Columbia Branch opened 1915

Fremont Branch opened 1921

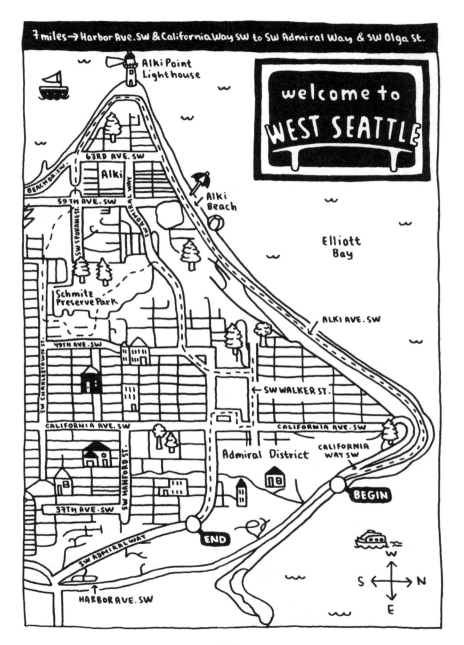

welcome to
WEST SEATTLE

Alki Point
Lighthouse

63RD AVE. SW

Alki

BEACH DR. SW

59TH AVE. SW

Alki
Beach

SW ADMIRAL WAY

SW SPOKANE ST.

Elliott
Bay

Schmitz
Preserve Park

ALKI AVE. SW

SW CHARLESTOWN ST.

49TH AVE. SW

← SW WALKER ST.

CALIFORNIA AVE. SW

CALIFORNIA AVE. SW

Admiral District

CALIFORNIA
WAY SW

SW HANFORD ST.

BEGIN

37TH AVE. SW

END

SW ADMIRAL WAY

↑
HARBOR AVE. SW

W
S ←→ N
E

PEOPLE USING LEAF BLOWERS:	|||| |||| ||||

COFFEE-CUP LIDS:	|||| |||| |||| ||||

JUST LOOK AT HOW ADORABLE THIS LITTLE FREE LIBRARY ON 44TH AVE. SW IS! IT'S A TINY ADMIRAL THEATRE!

47 locks on Admiral Way barrier:

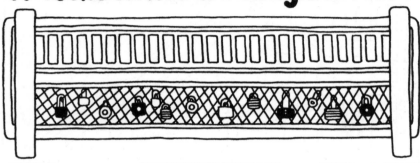

SPOTTED: a starfish AND a crab at the Charles Richey Sr. Viewpoint!

YEAH!

TREASURES OF ALKI

The Alki Point Lighthouse

The West Seattle Water Taxi

The Flower Houses on Alki Ave. SW

Schmitz Preserve Park's
MATCH THAT FOLIAGE!

West Seattle's Schmitz Preserve Park is a delightful old-growth forest with some of the city's finest trees. Can you match these lovely leaves with their home trees? Check your work on page 157!

ABIES GRANDIS
grand fir

THUJA PLICATA
western red cedar

TSUGA HETEROPHYLLA
western hemlock

PSEUDOTSUGA MENZIESII
Douglas fir

What's on the Sewer Grate?

← a juice box

a child's drawing and leaves →

← one flip-flop

SEAWEED STAIRS

The stairs at Alki Beach Park are a delightful seaweed wonderland during low tides.

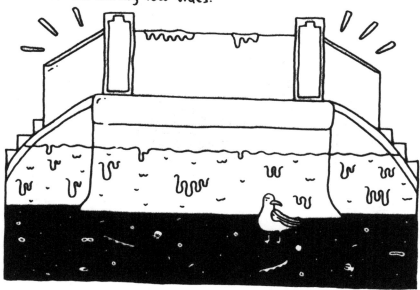

A Short Walk Down SW Walker St

an interesting house

a squirrel

a paper clip →

⧉ ← a bread tag

a kid practicing recorder

↑ a lovely garden

← a husky

an envelope

a very smooth rock

a leaf with a face →

a garden gnome

BETTER KNOW A SIGN!

NAME The "Drug Free Zone" Sign

BIRTHDAY May 31, 1990

NEIGHBORHOOD OF ORIGIN West Seattle

DESIGNED BY The City of Seattle's Engineering Department

BACKGROUND In 1990, Denny Middle School was the first school in Seattle to be given "Drug Free Zone" signs, now an inescapable but overlooked part of Seattle's streets.

The drug-free-zone program was created by Mayor Norm Rice and promoted a then-new Washington law that increased the penalty for dealing drugs around schools.

Whereas most Seattle signs are free from unnecessary adornments, the yellow-and-black "Drug Free Zone" signs feature a sassy line design.

THE OLDEST BUILDINGS IN SEATTLE

The Ward House, 1882
520 E. Denny Way on Capitol Hill

Both of these structures were built before Washington was officially recognized as a state in the Union!

The Korn Building, 1889
101 Occidental Ave. S. in Pioneer Square

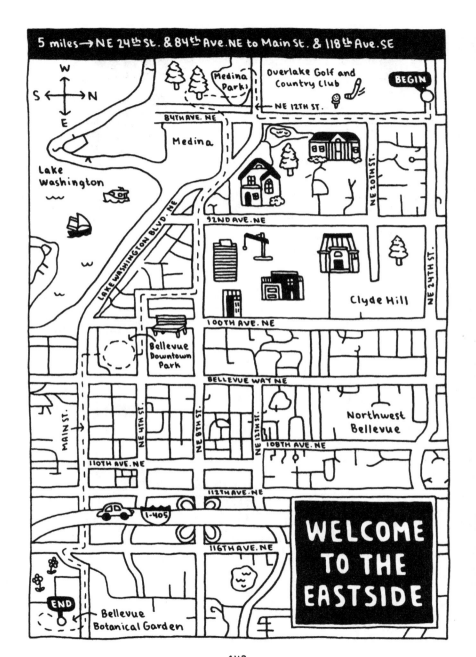

TREE-MENDOUS TREES

These trees on 98ᵗʰ Ave. NE look like they're having a team meeting!

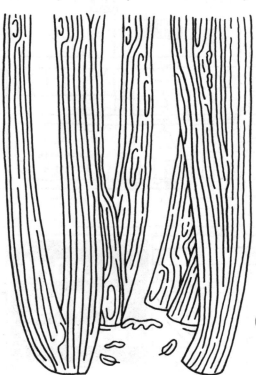

This former tree now sports a fashionable four-way birdhouse.

UNUSUAL SKYLINE SHAPES

St. Thomas Episcopal Church spire in Medina

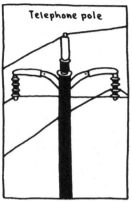

Telephone pole

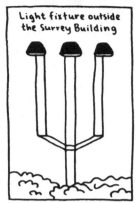

Light fixture outside the Surrey Building

BELLEVUE SIDEWALK-TREASURE HALL OF FAME

Wig and a glue stick

A beach ball shaped like a tennis ball

WHOA! Bellevue has exciting pedestrian-signal-button configurations you won't find in Seattle!

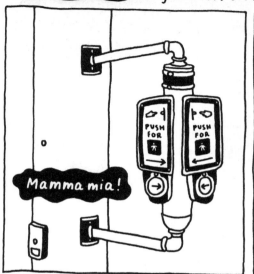

147

EASTSIDE HORRORS

A City of Clyde Hill cone... IN DOWNTOWN BELLEVUE!

One lonesome Wiffle ball!

A house with a single-car garage!

A marker indicating a property border in Medina... But the property's fence extends about 6 inches beyond it!

Bellevue Downtown Park

ACRES IN PARK: ~~HHT~~ ~~HHT~~ ~~HHT~~ ~~HHT~~ I

WOODEN BENCHES I COUNTED: ~~HHT~~ ~~HHT~~ ~~HHT~~ ~~HHT~~
~~HHT~~ ~~HHT~~ ~~HHT~~ ~~HHT~~ ~~HHT~~ ~~HHT~~ ~~HHT~~ ~~HHT~~ ~~HHT~~ ~~HHT~~ ~~HHT~~ ~~HHT~~
~~HHT~~ ~~HHT~~ ~~HHT~~ IIII

THAT'S 4.95 BENCHES PER ACRE!

Popular bench activities:

☑ Eating lunch

☑ Enjoying quality phone time

☑ Having a quiet afternoon cry

Spotted: → a Pomeranian

a bichon frise ↗

a cool streetlamp →

Seattle Walk Report's
Three Tenets for Walking Success

① Be open to possibility.

Part of the joy of walking is spontaneously deciding to veer down side streets you've overlooked or using a sidewalk closure as an opportunity to change the course of your walk. You never know what you may find down a street just a block away from where you started.

② Be safe.

If something feels off for any reason at all, do something else! It's important to listen to your body and trust your instincts about your environment. Use common sense when crossing streets or when walking in unfamiliar places.

③ Let go of any notion that there is a right way or wrong way to take a walk.

All walks, whether they last for five minutes or five miles, have the potential to be great experiences.

CONCLUSION

This may be the end of "Seattle Walk Report," but if you're not already a walking enthusiast, your adventures could begin today! I hope this book has inspired you to get out and see all that your neighborhood and city have to offer.

To make this book, I walked more than 65 miles through Seattle neighborhoods. Even in neighborhoods I knew well, discoveries were waiting around every corner. That's part of the magic of walking—every day, even blocks from where you live, there is something strange, novel, or mysterious waiting for you to find. You just need to slow down and take the time to see it!

The most difficult part of starting to walk recreationally is taking the first step. If you read walking guide books too closely, you might feel that if you don't follow the provided routes exactly, you'll miss out on what you're "supposed to" see. Before I was a walker, that fear of missing out prevented me from even trying. Then I realized that every one of my walking trips could start right outside my front door and take me anywhere I had the time and stamina to go.

Try finding your favorite tree!
This one on 3ʳᵈ Ave.W. and W. Lee St. in
Queen Anne captured my heart.

Here are a few ideas if you're feeling motivated to walk but don't know where to start:

- If you frequently walk a particular route to a nearby destination, like a grocery store or library, shift your route one block over and see what you find.

- Declare yourself the official walk reporter for your block. Find your favorite front door, mailbox, or tree. Count the number of cracks in the sidewalk or the different fence styles you see.

- Start walking in any direction. When you reach an intersection, flip a coin. Heads, you go left; tails, you go right.

Disclaimer: Seattle Walk Report is not responsible for causing you to walk into Lake Washington or an active construction site. Be careful out there.

xoxo, Seattle Walk Report

Search & Find

There are lots of objects hidden in the illustrations of this book! Can you find them all?

Four 4-leaf clovers	A grumpy seagull

A group of ants having the time of their lives

A bucket	A lost set of keys

2 apple cores

3 dental flossers

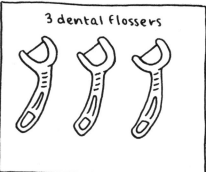

A take-out bag blowing in the wind

A hopscotch board

PSST! The answers are on the next page!

Answers to Search&Find

Four 4-leaf clovers
pages 22, 58, 125 & 146

A grumpy seagull
page 137

A group of ants having the time of their lives
page 92

☑ pigeons on the hunt for food
☑ neat architecture

A bucket
page 42

☑ tourists direction
☑ interest trash
☑ artistic

A lost set of keys
page 34

2 apple cores
pages 19 & 114

3 dental flossers
pages 2, 62 & 109

A take-out bag blowing in the wind
page 76

THANK YOU THANK YOU THANK YOU THANK YOU

A hopscotch board
page 85

ANSWERS TO THE DRINKING FOUNTAIN POP QUIZ! (page 70)

① B. There are 211 public drinking fountains in Seattle.

② C. Woodland Park has 11 public drinking fountains. Seward Park has 9. Discovery Park has 2.

③ A. Wedgwood has no public drinking fountains. Columbia City has 5. Alki has 2.

Metro Route 7 Maze Answer (page 116)

START →

You made a wrong turn and ended up getting lost in TUKWILA!

Someone decided to eat sardines on the bus, and now it needs to be evacuated!

You got a flat tire! All the passengers are mad at you!

← FINISH

You did it!

Match That Foliage Answer (page 136)

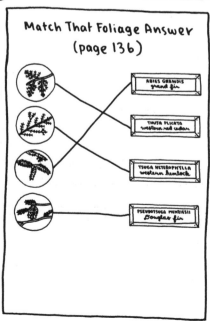

ABIES GRANDIS
grand fir

THUJA PLICATA
western red cedar

TSUGA HETEROPHYLLA
western hemlock

PSEUDOTSUGA MENZIESII
Douglas fir

157

Walking Supplies

If you've never walked for fun before, I encourage you to just start and see where your feet can take you. You don't need anything fancy... You just need yourself!

However, if you find that walking is consuming more and more of your life, I have some recommendations for a few items that are worth the investment.

Shoes!

The right pair of shoes with supportive insoles is the best thing you can buy to be a happy, healthy walker. I recommend going to a local running-shoe store to get a proper fitting and suggestions based on your activity level and walking style.

Wool socks!

To avoid blisters, give wool socks a try! Cotton has a tendency to make your feet super sweaty and give the sweat nowhere to go, which causes blisters. When I made the switch to wool socks, I was able to walk comfortably for longer periods of time and had less foot pain the day after a walk. I also stash an extra pair of socks in my bag when taking longer walks, just in case.

A waterproof jacket!

To survive walking in the rain, look for a waterproof jacket! I prefer jackets with large hoods over umbrellas so that my arms can stay free for tallying rainy-day dogs.

extra socks →

← snacks

sunscreen

sunglasses

← ibuprofen

a water bottle

an emergency library card →

your grandmother's antique compass (just for aesthetic purposes)

a finely tuned 6th sense for the presence of nearby dogs

a pencil and a notepad

tissues

a hat →

I've found that a backpack is the way to go when walking long distances! →

INDEX

Arched entryways: 4, 40, 41, 56, 64, 99, 124, 130, 131

Arson: 97

Balloons: 44, 75

Benches: 68, 84, 86, 109, 125, 149

Birdhouses: 25, 144

Bridges: 27, 50-51, 87, 117

Bus shelters: 25, 86

Churches: 86, 103, 145

Churros: 59

Coffee cups: 15, 54, 64, 134

Dogs: 12, 17, 19, 24, 34, 49, 65, 66, 74, 85, 108, 114, 138, 149

	Dressers: 9, 59
	Drinking fountains: 34, 70-71, 157
	Ducks (baby size): 17
	Ducks (normal size): 86, 115
	Fire hydrants: 17, 66
	Fire stations: 28, 124
	Food scraps that belong in the compost: VIII, 19, 24, 57, 66, 68, 79, 92
	Garfield High School: 24, 25
	The Gum Wall: 46, 48
	Hats: 88, 109, 125, 129, 159
	Houses: 4, 135, 138, 148
	Jaywalkers: 4

Jubilant exclamations: 16, 34, 87, 103, 124, 134, 146

Kids: 49, 58, 103, 138

King Country Metro: 116, 126

Libraries (normal size): 8, 22, 44, 84, 128, 130–131

Libraries (Little Free): 15, 24, 109, 134

Locks: 7, 134

Mount Rainier: 29, 42, 112, 127

Mountain Dew: 125

National Treasures: 37
(see also DOGS)

Ottomans: 9, 25

Overheard: 17, 39, 46, 58

Paper airplanes: 39

	Paper cups: 15, 64
	Parks: 10-11, 16, 17, 29, 34, 67, 68, 70, 71, 84, 86, 94, 97, 110, 111, 117, 129, 136, 137, 146, 149
	Plastic baggies: 15, 34
	QFC: 39, 68
	Question marks: 28, 34, 41, 46, 50, 57, 60, 61, 64, 67, 70, 76, 78, 79, 84, 89, 90, 94, 95, 100, 114, 116, 125, 136, 137, 154
	Raccoons: 19, 54
	Roundabouts: 74, 118
	Salty snacks: 24, 57
	Shoes: 14, 26, 94, 124, 129, 137
	Tallies: 4, 14, 17, 24, 34, 44, 54, 64, 74, 84, 94, 95, 103, 114, 124, 134, 144, 149
	Terra-cotta: 25, 41, 68, 105
	Things that look like turtles: 69, 74

	Topiaries: 54, 68
	Traffic cones: 25, 94, 114, 124, 148
	University of Washington: 30-31
	Utility poles: 55, 76, 119
	Vegetables: VIII, 61, 68, 79
	Vehicles: 5, 14, 39, 69, 75, 84, 103, 116, 126
	Viewpoints: 10, 16, 29, 134
	The Wedgwood Rock: 75, 100
	The word "wow": 101
	The letter "X": VII, X, 2, 8, 9, 22, 24, 28, 30, 38, 44, 45, 46, 50, 52, 57, 61, 72, 90, 100, 101, 102, 105, 107, 110, 120, 121, 122, 125, 126, 129, 131, 132, 135, 145, 147, 148, 150, 151, 153, 155, 158, 159
	Yard sales: 24, 76
	ZZZs (catching some): 49, 103

Susanna Ryan, a.k.a. Seattle Walk Report, is a lifelong Seattleite. She has never had a driver's license.